Mythologies

Giants

John Malam

QED

QED Publishing

Copyright © QED Publishing 2009

First published in the UK in 2009 by
QED Publishing
A Quarto Group company
226 City Road
London EC1V 2TT

A catalogue record for this book is available from
the British Library.

ISBN 978 1 84835 264 3

Author John Malam
Editor Amanda Learmonth
Designer Lisa Peacock
Illustrator Fernando Molinaro

Publisher Steve Evans
Creative Director Zeta Davies
Managing Editor Amanda Askew

Printed and bound in China

Picture credits
(t=top, b=bottom, l=left, r=right, c=centre, fc=front cover)
Alamy Images 9 Michael Runkel Greece, 11 Mary Evans
Picture Library, 12b Pictorial Press Ltd, 13 Mary Evans
Picture Library, 19t INTERFOTO Pressebildagentur,
21b Redmond Durrell, 22b Tony Watson, 23t Malcolm Park
London Events, 25b David Lyons
Bridgeman Art Library 17 Nationalmuseum, Stockholm,
Sweden
Corbis 4 Historical Picture Library
Getty Images 29b Photographer's Choice/Pamela E Reed
Mary Evans Picture Library 5tr, 5tl, 12t, 16t Edwin Wallace
Photoshot 7 De Agostini, 16b World Pictures
Shutterstock 23b Timo Kohlbacher, 25t Joe Gough
Topham Picturepoint 5tc Fortean/Svensson, 5cc Fortean/
Svensson, 27t Fortean Picture Library

Words in **bold** are explained
in the glossary on page 30.

CONTENTS

The world of giants

↑ *In the Bible story, David (right) challenges the mighty Goliath in battle.*

The myths and legends of the world are full of stories about giants and giantesses. These are massive creatures with great strength, but their huge size is not matched by big brains.

Giants tend to be rather slow-witted and can be easily fooled. This is their greatest weakness. They might be able to throw huge rocks and shake the ground with their footsteps, but a human will always outsmart a giant.

There have been many **races** of giant, and most of them lived when the world was very young. As time passed, the giants fought and lost battles. The few that survived were thrown into prisons, or went into hiding.

Big and bigger

There is an ancient Jewish story about a very tall man called Goliath. He was nearly 3 metres tall – much taller than everyone else! The word 'goliath' is now used to describe big things, from giant beetles to huge trucks.

Who's who among the giants?

Trolls
Trolls are gruesome creatures that guard treasure in underground places.

Jotun
These are giants of the air, frost, mountains and water.

Gigantes (Greek giants)
Gigantes are terrible, violent creatures with snakes' bodies for legs.

Ogres
Ogres are similar to trolls, but are scarier and much more beastlike.

Cyclopes
These are savage monsters, each with a single eye in its forehead.

Fomorians
These are monsters with vile bodies. Each one has a leg, an arm, an eye and three rows of teeth.

Centimanes
Three hideous brothers, each with 50 heads and 100 arms.

5

Giants of ancient Greece

▲ *A **Hundred-Hander**, a Gigante and a Cyclops — three giants of ancient Greece.*

The ancient Greeks believed in many different kinds of giant, and told wonderful stories about them. The greatest of these monstrous creatures were known as the Gigantes.

They were strong and dangerous, and had long, untidy hair. Instead of legs, they slithered about on the bodies of huge snakes. Stories explained that the Gigantes were the children of Gaia, the Earth goddess. Gaia was angry because her other children had been taken from her by new gods that lived on Mount Olympus.

One-eyed giants

In the myths of ancient Greece, the Cyclopes were three ugly giants. Each Cyclops had a single eye in the middle of its forehead. Their name means 'round-eyed'.

The Cyclopes lived beneath the volcano, Mount Etna, on the island of Sicily in southern Italy.

In revenge, she created the Gigantes. As soon as they were created, the Gigantes began to help their mother. She ordered them to destroy the **Olympian** gods, and there was a terrible war.

← Mount Olympus is said to be home to the gods of ancient Greece.

HUNDRED -HANDED GIANTS

The Centimanes were three giants with 50 heads and 100 hands. Their name means 'hundred-handed'. They were the brothers of the Cyclopes, and they guarded prisoners of the gods.

The Giants tossed boulders and burning trees at the gods, but their efforts came to nothing. Despite their great strength, they had a serious weakness.

They could be killed if a human fought with the gods – and that's what happened. A human called Heracles (say: *heh-ra-cleez*) helped the gods, and, one by one, the Gigantes were defeated.

➡ *Heracles and the gods of ancient Greece destroyed the terrible Gigantes using huge rocks, **thunderbolts** and arrows.*

Once upon a time:
How Odysseus tricked the Cyclops

• GREECE

It's Nobody!

Odysseus told Polyphemus that his name was 'Nobody'. When Polyphemus was blinded, he cried out in pain. Other Cyclopes asked who was attacking him, and because Polyphemus said it was 'Nobody', the giants went away.

Long ago, there was a giant called Polyphemus (say: pol-ee-feem-oos). He was a Cyclops – a fierce, one-eyed monster.

One day, Odysseus (*say: o-dee-see-oos*), who was a Greek hero, visited an island and came to Polyphemus' cave. He went inside and found a flock of sheep. When the giant saw Odysseus, he blocked the cave entrance with a boulder. Odysseus was trapped inside, and feared for his life.

← *The blinded Polyphemus searched his cave for Odysseus.*

That night, as Polyphemus slept, Odysseus stabbed him in the eye and made him blind. Then, he hid from Polyphemus by clinging onto the belly of a sheep. The blinded Polyphemus stumbled and felt around the cave for Odysseus.

As long as the giant's fingers touched only the soft, woolly back of the sheep, Odysseus knew he was safe. After a while, Polyphemus moved the boulder away from the cave entrance. His flock ran from the cave to their pasture, and that is how the cunning Odysseus escaped to safety.

⬆ Odysseus escaped to safety by clinging to the belly of a sheep.

⬇ The ancient city of Tiryns, Greece, is surrounded by a wall of giant blocks of stone.

Built by giants

The ancient Greeks thought the walls of some of their oldest cities had been built by giants. They believed that only giants had the strength to move such massive stones. Ancient walls such as this are called **Cyclopean** walls.

Once upon a time:
The war against the Gigantes

• GREECE

This myth comes from…

Of all the heroes of ancient Greece, there was none greater than Heracles. A war was looming between the gods of Mount Olympus and the Gigantes.

The gods could not defeat the Gigantes without help from a human, and as Heracles had more courage than any other **mortal**, they chose him.

The god Zeus struck down Porphyrion with a thunderbolt.

The Gigantes lived among the volcanoes of a place called the **Burning Lands**. This is where the greatest battle of the war was fought. The strongest of all the Gigantes were the brothers Alcyoneus (say: *al-ky-on-ee-oos*) and Porphyrion (say: *por-fy-ree-on*).

As they moved towards the gods, the Gigantes hurled massive rocks at them. When Alcyoneus was within range, Heracles shot him with a poisoned arrow. The monster came crashing down. He was hurt, but as long as he stayed within the Burning Lands, he could not die. Heracles dragged him away, and once they were beyond the Burning Lands, Alcyoneus was destroyed.

Next came Porphyrion. He was in a fearful rage, but the great god Zeus struck him down with a thunderbolt thrown from the heavens. Then the poisoned arrows of Heracles finished him off.

⬆ Brought down by a thunderbolt from Zeus, Porphyrion lay on the ground where the poisoned arrows of Heracles killed him.

⬇ Heracles killed the Hydra monster to use its poisonous blood on his arrow-tips.

Poisoned arrows

The poison that Heracles used against the Gigantes came from the Hydra. This was a monster in the shape of a giant serpent with many heads. Heracles killed the Hydra and cut open its body. He then took its poisonous blood to use as venom on his arrow-tips.

Odious ogres, hideous hags

Giants appear in many fairy tales from Europe, where the men are called ogres and the women are called **hags**. In many cases they are simply known as 'beasts', and for good reason.

Ogres and hags look like humans, but are much bigger in size. They are incredibly strong, but they are also stupid, slow-moving and very ugly. The worst thing about them is their taste for human flesh, and that's what makes them so very scary.

◄ *Shrek the ogre gets his name from the German word* schreck, *meaning 'terror'.*

▲ *Artists have always pictured a hag, or crone, as a wrinkled old woman.*

An ogre is born

Ogres are still being invented today. In 2001, the lead role in the movie 'Shrek' was an ogre. But Shrek the ogre is a friendly character, very different from the ogres in traditional stories.

From bones to bread

The giant in the well-known fairy tale 'Jack and the Beanstalk' is a human-gobbling ogre. He promises to turn poor Jack's bones into powder, which he'll use to make his bread:

'Fee! Fie! Foe! Fum!
I smell the blood of an Englishman.
Be he alive, or be he dead,
I'll grind his bones to make my bread.'

⬆ *In the fairy tale 'Jack and the Beanstalk',
Jack stole a magic harp from the giant.*

Anyone for a hag's dish?

Haggis is a traditional food from Scotland, made with meat and spices. No one knows how haggis got its name. One idea is that it means 'hag's dish' – a mix of body parts eaten by bloodthirsty hags!

Hags can live for a very long time, which is why they are called Old Hags or Undying Hags. One hag called Black Annis (or Black Agnes) is said to live in a cave in the Dane Hills, near Leicester, England. She has a blue face, yellow teeth and long, iron claws. At dusk, she leaves her cave and hunts humans who have stayed out too late on the hills. Once in her grip, a poor soul is gobbled up.

Once upon a time:
Baba Yaga and Vasilisa the Brave

CZECH
REPUBLIC • • POLAND
• RUSSIA

This myth comes from…

There was once a lovely young girl called Vasilisa, whose evil stepmother was always cruel to her.

One day, the candle in Vasilisa's house went out, and her stepmother told her to bring fire from Baba Yaga, the woman who lived in the woods. Baba Yaga was a horrible old hag, and Vasilisa was frightened of her.

⬆ *Baba Yaga was a crooked old hag who flew around the woods in a grinding bowl.*

Now, before Vasilisa's real mother died, she gave her a magic wooden doll. As Vasilisa made her way to Baba Yaga's house, the doll spoke and said she would not let any harm come to her. Vasilisa came to a clearing in the woods, and there was the hag's strange-looking house. It was whirling around on hens' legs! The old hag took Vasilisa inside, and from then on she was a prisoner.

Each day, Baba Yaga set her tasks, saying that if they weren't done, she would eat the girl for tea. When the old hag wasn't looking, Vasilisa's doll helped her. When asked how she had done the work, Vasilisa said, "By my mother's love." Baba Yaga hated the mention of 'love', and told Vasilisa to take the fire she had come for and go home.

Vasilisa left. The fire she took glowed from inside a skull. When her wicked stepmother saw it, she burst into flames! From then on, Vasilisa was free to live as she wished.

One look at Baba Yaga's flame and Vasilisa's evil stepmother burst into flames.

THE BONY-LEGGED ONE

Baba Yaga is also known as the Bony-Legged One. She is described as a flesh-eating hag with fangs and a hooked nose. Her gaze can turn people to stone. She flies around in a mortar (a bowl used for grinding food).

Giants of northern lands

The lands of Scandinavia and northern Europe are rich in stories about giants. Long ago, this region was the home of the **Vikings**, who told amazing tales of the Jotun (say: yo-tun), or giants.

Viking stories say the Jotun existed at the very beginning of time, and were the first living things on Earth. The Jotun made the world a very dangerous place to live.

⬆ *A Frost Giant – one of the mighty Jotun.*

⬅ *The snowy mountains of **Jotunheim**, or Giantland, are said to be home to the Jotun.*

Giantland

In Norway there is a region known as Jotunheim (say: yo-tun-hime), meaning 'Giantland'. This is where the Jotun are said to live, among the cold, snow-covered mountains.

The Jotun looked like humans, but with massive bodies. They could be very ugly. Some, such as Thrivaldi ('Thrice Mighty') had many heads – he had nine in total. They lived in mountain caves in icy places. Sometimes the Jotun were helpful to humans, but they also had bad tempers.

The Jotun are divided into four groups – Air Giants, such as Kari (meaning 'Tempest'), Frost Giants, such as Thrym ('Frost'), Water Giants, such as Gymir ('Sea'), and Mountain Giants, such as Senjeman from the island of Senjen.

Terrible trolls

Scandinavia is also home to creatures called trolls. Some are as big as giants, others are tiny. They are all ugly and hairy with hunched backs. They live underground, where they guard valuable treasures. If the Sun shines on them, they are turned to stone.

← *Trolls live in underground places, where they guard great treasures.*

Once upon a time:
Why Thrym took the magic hammer

ICELAND •   • SCANDINAVIA

This myth comes from...

Thor was the mightiest of the Viking gods. He defended both gods and humans against the Jotun, or giants. But this was only possible as long as his magic hammer, Mjöllnir (say: me-yoll-near), was with him.

The Jotun knew that the secret of Thor's power lay in his great hammer, so they plotted to steal it. Thrym, a Frost Giant, took Mjöllnir, and he buried it in the land of the giants.

➡ *The giant Thrym was easily fooled by Thor's clever plan.*

LUCKY CHARM

Thor's Hammer, or Mjöllnir, was made by **dwarfs** in their underground workshops. Viking men and women often carried tiny copies of Mjöllnir as lucky charms to keep them safe from harm.

➡ *A Viking lucky charm, made in the shape of Thor's Hammer.*

Thor shook with anger to find that Mjöllnir had gone. He asked the god Loki to help him find it. Loki went to Thrym, who said they could only have the hammer in exchange for the goddess Freyja (say: *fray-a*). Thor decided to trick Thrym, for he knew that all giants could be easily fooled.

Thor dressed as a bride and pretended to be Freyja. With his face behind a veil, he went to Thrym. A great wedding feast was set. Thrym called for Mjöllnir, and when it was placed in Thor's hand he turned it on the giant and struck him dead. From then on, Mjöllnir was known as Thor's Hammer, and the two were never parted again.

Once upon a time:
The trolls in Hedal Woods

• NORWAY

This myth comes from…

Two brothers were out walking in Hedal Woods, in Norway. It grew late, and darkness fell quickly. The boys realized they were trapped among the trees.

They gathered branches and made a shelter for the night. They had barely closed their eyes when they heard a snuffling and a scuffling from outside. The noises grew louder and the ground began to shake. The boys knew that the three trolls of Hedal Woods were upon them.

⬇ *The older brother chased after the trolls with a knife.*

The trolls shared one eye between them. Each troll had a hole in its forehead, and whoever placed the eye in its socket was the only one that could see. The seeing troll led the way, and the blind trolls followed.

The younger brother ran, and the trolls chased him. The older brother came after the trolls and chopped the ankle of the slowest one. It screamed, and this gave the seeing troll such a fright that it dropped the eye.

↑ The trolls pleaded with the boys to give back their precious eye.

← Mistletoe is a poisonous plant that grows on and lives off a tree or a shrub.

The boys picked up the trolls' eye, and all three trolls let out a roar as loud as thunder. The brothers let them roar, for they knew that as long as the trolls could not see, they were safe.

Keeping trolls away

Trolls are said to steal women, children, animals and belongings. Humans can protect themselves from the trolls by placing mistletoe around their house.

The trolls pleaded with the brothers, and agreed to give them gold and silver in return for their eye. They also promised never to harm anyone else that wandered into Hedal Woods.

Giants of Britain and Ireland

It was once believed that all of Britain and Ireland was home to giants.

In Britain there were three brothers – Albion, Gog and Magog – who, so ancient stories say, were defeated by an invading army of humans. In Ireland, a race of giants known as the Fomorians were said to have first lived on the island.

The Fomorians were hideous creatures with human bodies, the heads of goats, and only one eye, one arm and one leg each. All of Ireland was theirs, but in time they were defeated in battle and they disappeared.

◄ *The Fomorians were gruesome giants from Ireland.*

▼ *The Long Man of Wilmington is a giant figure cut into the white chalk of a hill.*

Chalk giant

Carved into a hill near the village of Wilmington, England, is a giant known as the Long Man of Wilmington. He is 69 metres tall! A story says that an enemy giant knocked him over, and the outline of his body was cut into the hill where he fell.

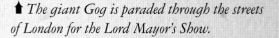

The giant Gog is paraded through the streets of London for the Lord Mayor's Show.

Giants on parade

The City of London is said to be guarded by the giants Gog and Magog. Since the 1500s, giant-sized figures of them have been paraded each year at the Lord Mayor's Show.

As for Albion, Gog and Magog, the memory of them did not die with them. For hundreds of years, Britain was known as 'Albion'. Statues of Gog and Magog were put up outside the Guildhall, the City of London's town hall.

Some say the ancient stone circle of Stonehenge, England, was built by giants.

STONE CIRCLE

Stonehenge is an ancient stone circle in Wiltshire, England. It was once known as the Giants' Dance. Legend says it was built by giants, who placed it on a mountain in Ireland, and then later it was brought to England.

Once upon a time:
How Finn McCool fooled Fingal

This myth comes from…

• IRELAND

Finn McCool was a giant who came from Ireland. He lived on a headland that poked out into the sea, in the direction of Scotland.

Finn McCool hurled boulders across the sea to make a pathway for him to walk on.

One day, a Scottish giant called Fingal spied Finn McCool from across the water. Fingal called Finn McCool names and this made the Irish giant very angry.

Finn McCool took up a great clump of soil and hurled it at Fingal. It missed, and splashed into the sea. Fingal laughed, and tossed back a massive rock.

The Giant's Causeway

The Giant's Causeway is an area of Northern Ireland that is made up of amazing rock formations. These were caused millions of years ago by volcanic eruptions.

➡ *The Giant's Causeway stretches out to sea as far as the Scottish island of Staffa. In the story of Finn McCool, this is the pathway he made.*

⬆ *Fingal's Cave, on the island of Staffa, Scotland.*

This only made Finn McCool angrier, and for the next week he hurled rock after rock into the sea, until he had made a great pathway that joined Ireland to Scotland. Now the giants could fight each other face to face.

Fingal's Cave

The Scottish end of the Giant's Causeway is on the island of Staffa. A cave on the island is called Fingal's Cave, which is where Fingal is said to be in hiding.

But, by now, Finn McCool was too tired to go to Fingal. So he came up with a plan. He dressed as a baby and lay down in a cot. When Fingal stormed across to Finn McCool's house, he saw what he thought was a baby. If the baby is as big as a giant, he thought, how much bigger Finn McCool must be! And with this, Fingal fled back to Scotland and hid inside a cave.

Giants of America

Giants have a special place in the traditional stories of the Native Americans of Canada and the USA. There are tales of giants that are kind to humans, and others that are to be feared, such as the **Sasquatch** and the Coeur d'Alene Tree Men.

⬇ The Coeur d'Alene people lived in fear of the Tree Men.

Stories of giants known as Tree Men come from the Coeur d'Alene people. This tribe's homeland is now made up of the US states of Idaho, eastern Washington and western Montana. Taller than teepees, the Tree Men were hairy and had a bad smell. They could change into trees or bushes, and they ate fish, which they stole from people's traps.

Helpful giant

The Iroquois people of northeastern USA tell tales of a helpful giant called Split-Face. His body is red on one side and black on the other. He protects people from evil.

CAUGHT ON FILM

In 1967, Roger Patterson and Robert Gimlin said they had filmed a **Bigfoot** in California, USA. To this day, no one is sure if the film really does show a giant, hairy animal or if it's just a man dressed up as Bigfoot.

▲ *This photograph may show Bigfoot — but it could be a fake.*

The native peoples of western Canada and northwest USA tell stories of a giant creature that walks like a man and is covered in long, shaggy hair. Some stories say it stands 4.5 metres tall. It has many names, but Sasquatch, meaning 'wild man', is the one that now joins them all together. A more popular name for it is Bigfoot.

Once upon a time:
Paul Bunyan, the giant lumberjack

• USA

This myth comes from…

There was once a baby boy named Paul Bunyan. He was so big he wore his father's clothes, and his cry was so loud that frogs jumped from their ponds.

On his first birthday, Paul's father gave him a blue ox named Babe. As Paul grew, so did Babe, and soon everyone knew about the giant boy and his giant ox.

When Paul became a man, he took a job as a **lumberjack**. He worked all day with seven big, strong axemen, cutting down trees with one swing of his axe.

➤ *Paul Bunyan and his axemen at work.*

One year, it was so cold it felt as if there were two winters. Paul worked right through. When he spoke, his words froze in mid-air. When the air thawed out in the spring, his chattering voice was heard for weeks.

▲ Paul Bunyan worked hard through the long, cold winter.

All-American hero
The tales of Paul Bunyan were first told in the late 1800s. They proved so popular that today he is something of an all-American hero. A few towns have put up giant statues in his honour.

He used giant mosquitoes to drill holes in wood, and giant worker ants to haul logs from the forest. No task was ever too big for Paul Bunyan, and no deed was too difficult. If help was needed, Paul Bunyan, the giant lumberjack, would save the day.

◄ The Grand Canyon is 365 kilometres long, 29 kilometres wide and about 1.5 kilometres deep.

The Grand Canyon
The Grand Canyon is a huge, deep, rocky valley in Arizona, USA. It was said that Paul Bunyan created the Grand Canyon when he dragged his axe across the ground.

GLOSSARY

Bigfoot
A giant creature from the myths of western Canada and northwest USA. It is said to walk like a man and look like a huge, hairy animal. It is also known as a Sasquatch.

Burning Lands
A place where the Gigantes lived, among the burning hot volcanoes.

Cyclopean
An adjective used to describe a building or a wall that is so big it could have been built by giants.

Dwarfs
Hard-working fairies that live underground. Their special gift is to turn jewels and other riches into beautiful objects.

Hag
An ugly old female giant from the myths of Europe, also known as an ogress. A male is called an ogre. Hags are stupid creatures that are easily fooled by humans.

Haggis
A traditional food from Scotland. It is usually made from the chopped-up lungs, heart and liver of a sheep, mixed with onion, oatmeal, spices and salt.

Hundred-Handers
Another name for the Centimanes – giants from the myths of ancient Greece that each had 50 heads and 100 arms.

Jotunheim
A region in Norway where the Jotun, or giants, were said to live at the beginning of the world. The name means Giantland.

Lumberjack
Someone who cuts down trees for their job.

Mistletoe
A plant with white berries that grows on trees. It is a parasite – it lives off the tree it grows on, and can cause it harm.

Mortal
An ordinary human being who doesn't have any superhuman or magical powers.

Olympian
An adjective used to describe the gods of ancient Greece that lived on a mountain called Mount Olympus.

Race
The family to which a particular type of giant belongs.

Sasquatch
Also known as Bigfoot, this hairy giant is said to roam the wild parts of Canada and northwest USA. Its name means 'wild man'.

Stone circle
Large stones arranged so that they stand upright in a circle, made by the people of ancient Europe, particularly Britain and Ireland. The most famous stone circle in Britain is Stonehenge.

Thunderbolt
A lightning flash and a clap of thunder that happens together. In ancient Greece, Zeus, the king of the gods, had the power to throw thunderbolts down to Earth.

Vikings
A group of people that came from Scandinavia, in the north of Europe. The Viking Age began about 1200 years ago and lasted for 300 years.